You Have a Superpower

The Extraordinary Power of Unconditional Love

Odille Rault

You Have a Superpower
Copyright © 2014 by Odille Rault

Cover design by Azeema Fatima - contact.azeema@gmail.com

All rights reserved. No part of this book may be reproduced or transmitted in any form or by any means without written permission from the author.

ISBN-13: 978-1502876690
ISBN-10: 1502876698

Dedication

I dedicate this book to every one of my clients and the readers of my previous books, **THE MAGIC PILL**, **THE SECOND DOSE** and **BEYOND THE MAGIC PILL**, without whom I would not have been pushed to find many of the answers and solutions you will find here. It is through my own quest to improve my life that I discovered the superpower, but it is because of my clients and readers that I was inspired to find further answers, explanations and insights I would not have otherwise discovered.

This book is also dedicated to my sister, Sharelle Wodehouse for her amazing insight, brilliance, and encouragement. She is my voice of reason, my cheer leader and my oracle as well as my closest friend.

Finally, I dedicate "You Have a Superpower" to you. You are my reason for writing it. You are about to become a real life superhero, with your own infinite superpower. Have fun with it!

Table of Contents

Acknowledgements 7
Preface 9
Introduction 11
What is Unconditional Love? 13
Why Unconditional Love Works on Anything and Everything . 17
How Unconditional Love Works for Happiness 21
How Unconditional Love Works for Relationships .. 23
How Unconditional Love Works in the Work Place . 41
How Unconditional Love Works With Finances 53
How Unconditional Love Works With the Law of Attraction ... 62
Beginner's Exercise 75
Superpower Exercise 79
Technique for Using Your Superpower on Difficult and Negative People 83
Using Your Superpower to Heal Your Body 85
Using Your Superpower for Health........................ 91
Technique for Fear and Anxiety 93
Technique for "Broken" Things 97
Power Phrases.. 101
When You Can't Feel Love 105
More Techniques and Tips for Tuning In.............. 107
Points to Remember 109
In Closing 111

Acknowledgements

My discovery of the power of unconditional love came about through a combination of the information and techniques I learned from three particular sources, which led to my own interpretations and insight; and the result is the information I share with you in this book. I would like to acknowledge my appreciation for the three brilliant (and unwitting) contributors to this work:

- Abraham-Hicks - www.abraham-hicks.com
- Klaus Joehle (Living on Love)
  http://livingonlove.com/
- Joe Vitale (in particular, his information on Ho'oponopono)
  http://www.mrfire.com/

Through these three sources, I discovered and developed the Superpower of Unconditional Love, and I continue to enjoy and appreciate their work. I hope you will too!

I would also like to acknowledge two inspiring and remarkable people who have contributed a significant amount to my writing this book:

Jessica Fontana, one of my star clients, who has achieved miracles and magic using her superpower, and has been generous enough to allow me to share her achievements with the world.
and
Snigdha Jain, another of my star clients who has not only been a shiny example of what is possible using the power of unconditional love, but has also generously contributed her editorial expertise to the creation of this book.

Preface

When I first wrote **BEYOND THE MAGIC PILL** I had no idea that the most important part of that book would be the chapter on unconditional love. I had discovered the power of unconditional love by accident, and although I was using it with great success at that time, I could not have foreseen the remarkable potential of such a power. In the years since then, through my own experience as well as the experience of those I've coached, I have discovered so much more about this power that I realized it needs a book of its own! So, here it is. ☺

Introduction

You have a superpower! A real, genuine, tangible superpower. It's weird because we're all walking around with this massive power inside us, and no awareness that it's even there never mind how to use it. At first, it's difficult to believe it's there; and really, the only way to believe it is to start using it. Just start… and you'll surprise yourself!

I remember when my son was little, and had just watched the movie "The Incredibles". He was, naturally, fascinated by the family's superpowers. He asked me: if I could have any superpower in the world (only one) which would I choose. I seem to remember that he had chosen invisibility; I chose the ability to fly. Little did I realize at the time, I already possessed a superpower – much, much more powerful (and infinitely more versatile) than the ability to fly!

Years later, when I stumbled upon my own superpower, it took me quite some time to learn to use it effectively. As I practiced and developed my technique, I shared it with others, and was excited to hear that it worked for them too! Because I learned to use my superpower by trial and error, without a guide or manual, it took me a significant amount of time to become an expert in using it. However, through that journey, I developed a very simple strategy for learning to use the power.

The step-by-step techniques and exercises I created over the years are designed specifically for developing the skill that is needed in order to use this superpower effectively. This means you will be able to go from beginner to expert in a far shorter time-frame than I did! With practice and focus, you will be able to start using your superpower immediately.

The information in this book will introduce to you to your superpower and explain exactly how and why it works. I'm also including the exercises, techniques and tools that have enabled me, and my clients, to develop the skill and ability to use this power with incredible results – from the first tentative sensations… to manifesting dream jobs, happiness, relationship harmony, health, peace… and so much more!

It takes practice. It takes focus and practice, just like learning to ride a bike or learning any other skill; and through this book, I will hold your hand, guide you, encourage you, and even catch you when you fall. ☺ Just keep your eye on me, and keep going. Compare it to a skill you learned that took some time, focus and practice – perhaps riding a bike, playing an instrument, learning ballet, or surfing.

Learning to use your superpower is like learning any other skill. You'll start off tentatively, with "hit and miss" results while you learn to tune in; and as you stick to practicing every day, you will build your skill, and you will start to see more consistent results; and those results will grow into more powerful and impressive "miracles". I put the word "miracles" in quote marks because once you've become an expert in using your power, you will no longer see them as miracles – they will become perfectly normal. ☺

So, let's get started…

What is Unconditional Love?

To most of us, unconditional love is an emotion. Love without condition. It sounds soft and fuzzy; a passive emotion. This couldn't be further from the truth. Unconditional love is the name given to the sensation we feel when we are channeling our power. It's how we know we're tuned in to the energy that creates and transforms; the energy of which everything (and everyone) is made. Unconditional love is how the power of Source Energy, God, The Universe – whichever term suits you – feels.

When you first start to tune in to your superpower, you will use the feeling of unconditional love as a tool for getting aligned and tuned in; it's also your indication of when you are tuned into your power, and when you slip out of the frequency. Imagine you're standing in front of a table which has a number of sticks on it. They're all stick-shaped, but one of them is a magic wand. Because they all look the same, you can't tell by looking at them, which is the wand. The only way to tell is by picking them up.

When you pick up the wand, you'll feel a tingle through your hand; when you pick up a stick, you won't feel the tingle. The same goes for your power - when you are channeling your power, you will feel the sensation of unconditional love. If you don't feel that sensation (if the love feels conditional, for example) then you know that you're "holding a stick, not the wand" – and you'll need to keep feeling around for that "tingle".

Another analogy for using unconditional love as an indicator for when you're tuned in to your power is: Imagine a dark room. Somewhere in that room is a shower. The water runs constantly. You want to get under the shower, but you can't see it (let's pretend the water is silent as well ;)) and so you need to move around the room until you feel wet. When you feel wet, you know you're standing under the shower. When you no longer feel wet, you know you've moved away from it, so you move around again until you feel wet once more.

Now, in the beginning, the idea of loving something you don't want can seem crazy. It's natural to be concerned that by loving something, you are encouraging more of it. For example, if you love the fact that you have no money, wouldn't that mean you'd be accepting, and thereby encouraging, continuing lack of money? And if you unconditionally love someone who is negative – in fact, love them for their negativity – wouldn't that encourage them to continue being negative? Interestingly, no. ☺

It's a strange concept to wrap the brain around at first, but it will make sense as you go through this book. Here's a way that can help to explain it: I see unconditional love as light. When you shine light into light, it brightens the existing light. When you shine light into darkness, it transforms the darkness to light.

In the same way, when you love something you want (light) unconditionally, you create more of what you want; when you love something you don't want (darkness) unconditionally, your power transforms what you don't want into what you do want. Darkness cannot survive in light, but a light can shine in the dark. Unconditional love is your torch.

The potency of this power is in the "unconditional" bit – and that is the bit that can be challenging in the beginning. It's tricky at first, but with practice it becomes really, really easy. It helps to keep in mind this is not an emotion, it's an energy; a power.

It doesn't matter what you think because the skill you will develop, for using your power doesn't rely on thought. The method I'll teach you for accessing and using your power has nothing to do with your thoughts.

In fact, it is a great tool for changing your thoughts. Using your power is a physiological process you'll master; and once you've honed your skill, you will be able to "switch it on" right in the middle of negative thinking, and change your thinking from the inside out. With this power, you can easily (yup, easily) love something without agreeing with it; you can love someone without condoning his or her behavior. It only takes practice.

The more you practice, the easier it will get; your power will increase in potency, and you'll see the most remarkable results. As we go through this, I will show you exactly how to conjure your power, and how to develop it to the point where you can hold it for longer periods of time, until it becomes your dominant state.

Unconditional Love is the sensation we feel when we are tuned in to our Power

Why Unconditional Love Works on Anything and Everything

According to scientific experiments, detailed and explained by Gregg Braden (see the references at the back of this book, for details), not only is everything in this universe connected, and made of the same energy, but there is scientific proof that the electromagnetic activity of the heart – caused by emotion – directly affects our DNA.

The experiments proved that participants trained in feelings of love and compassion literally changed the shape of their DNA through these feelings. They weren't concentrating on changing their DNA, they were simply feeling the feelings of love and compassion (unconditional love), and their DNA changed automatically.

Scientists have also proven that human DNA affects the stuff everything in our universe is made of. Photons (light particles) isolated in a container, were arranged randomly, until human DNA was added to the container. The photons then assumed the shape of the DNA. In addition to this, when the DNA was removed, the photons remained in the shape of the DNA, showing that human DNA has a lasting effect on the world around it, on a quantum level.

So, in brief: How we feel affects the electromagnetic activity of our heart, which affects our DNA, which affects the building blocks of the world around us.

Gregg Braden also describes a meeting with an abbot in Tibet. He asked the wise man what the force is, that connects the universe and holds everything together. He had to ask the monk to repeat his reply through the translator, as he thought he'd heard it incorrectly. The reply was "Compassion". The Abbot confirmed that compassion is both a sensation we feel in our bodies, and the force that connects and holds the universe together.

Considering just the information from Gregg Braden here, you can see how feeling unconditional love (which of course includes compassion) has an effect on the world around you, on a scientific, quantum level.

Apart from the energetic, quantum and spiritual aspects of this power, there is also a physical, chemical result. What you feel affects your chemistry. When you feel love, "feel-good chemicals" are created and absorbed by the brain. This affects your state. Tuning in to your power, using unconditional love will change how you feel.

When you feel good, you behave differently to the way you behave when you're not feeling good – which, of course gives you different results in all areas of life.

When you feel good:

- You make different choices and decisions to those you make when you're feeling bad.
- You communicate differently.
- You behave differently.
- You relate to others differently.
- You respond to challenges differently when you're feeling good.
- You're more likely to take action towards goals and to get chores done.
- You're more likely to eat healthily and less likely to binge or eat junk food.

- You have more energy when you're feeling good, and are more likely to be physically active and exercise.
- The "feel-good chemicals" boost your immune system.
- You're also more aware, and notice more opportunities – and are more willing to make the most of them – when you're feeling good.
- You come across to others as more confident and competent when you're feeling good.

…. and the list goes on. You can see, from just this brief overview, how feeling good can affect the results you experience in all areas of your life, just on a purely down-to-earth physical level even without the quantum science, energy and law of attraction aspect.

The ability to conjure up the sensation of unconditional love will enable you to tune in to feeling good at any time, under any circumstances – which will enable you to get into a peak state on demand in order to make the best of your life regardless of what's going on around you.

How you feel affects how you act and respond, which affects the results you experience in all areas of your life.

How Unconditional Love Works for Happiness

Interestingly, you can feel unconditional love and unhappiness at the same time. You can feel fear and unconditional love at the same time. You can feel frustration, anger and irritation, and unconditional love at the same time. But as you start to feel unconditional love in the moment, in the middle of whatever negative emotions you're feeling at the time, your superpower neutralizes the negative state and replaces it.

Once you develop your power, you will be able to tune in to it on demand, in an instant, right in the middle of anything. Right in the middle of a negative situation, right in the middle of an argument, right in the middle of anxiety; and you will transform your emotional state into bliss. It's a skill. And it gets easier and more effective, the more you practice it.

The exercises I'll be sharing with you later in this book are designed to help you to develop your skill; and once you've mastered it, you'll no longer need to go through the exercise to access your power. You will be able to access your power instantly – to tune in to unconditional love, and aim it at anything, instantly.

Aiming the power of unconditional love at a negative experience is like drenching darkness in light. It changes not only how you feel, but your vibrational state as well. It changes the electro-magnetic activity of your heart, which in turn has a direct effect on the world around you. And again, with practice, you will be able to hold that state – to remain tuned in – for longer and longer periods of time, until it becomes your dominant state.

As you practice, you'll find you're not only using it more often, but you're able to sustain that state for longer periods of time, which will result in your spending more of your time feeling happy!

You don't need to get what you want in order to be happy; but you do need to be happy in order to get what you want.

How Unconditional Love Works for Relationships

When you consider we're all connected on a quantum level, and that the electromagnetic activity of our hearts affects the world around us, it's not a stretch to understand that this activity also affects the people around us. The vibrations of the heart expand as far as science has been able to measure – which is several feet. This means, of course, that you are constantly overlapping with other people, and your heart vibrations are therefore interacting with theirs.

We know that what we say is only a fraction of our communication with others. We know that both tone of voice and body language have a much more powerful effect, and convey far more information than our words communicate. And we know that all of this is mostly registered by the other person's subconscious. However, beyond body language is the energetic communication. Our energy is interacting with those around us, regardless of what we're saying and doing.

Now, because this is all "under the radar" – undetectable to the conscious mind – we are unaware it is going on; but it's still having an effect. Have you ever felt something about someone, and called it "a hunch"? Have you ever felt positive or negative feelings about someone you've only just met, with no logical explanation for these feelings? We affect each other, just as we affect everything else in the world around us, on an unseen energetic level, according to how we are vibrating – which is indicated by how we're feeling.

Of course, different feelings will create different vibrations, which will have varying results. As you can imagine, unconditional love is the most powerful positive energy that exists. If how we feel affects the results we get in life, imagine the effect of the power of unconditional love!

The exercises and techniques I'll share with you later in this book will help you to develop your power to the point where you will be able to completely change your experience with difficult and negative people. You will be able to aim your power at a negative or difficult person by conjuring up (using the techniques I'll teach you) unconditional love for them. You will be able to feel love for them regardless of what they do or say. You will be able to do this right in the middle of feeling annoyed, hurt, angry or frustrated; and you will be able to sustain it – to stay tuned in. The results will astound you!

I first discovered the potency of using the power of unconditional love in this way when I used it on a person I was having a very difficult time with. This was about 8 years ago, when I was still right in the beginning of my superpower discovery. That particular person had been spiteful and mean, and had done some terrible things, including lying in court. I didn't know how I was ever going to be able to forgive her, or even speak to her again; there was so much hurt and damage.

I decided to use my superpower, to test if it would work in a situation like this. To be perfectly honest, I didn't expect it to work on the other person at all; I was doing it simply to change my own perspective so that I could get past the pain. I chose to see this person as a spiritual being who was playing the role of a "baddie" in the story of my life. And at first, even though I couldn't forgive her, I could start by at least appreciating her performance! ☺ This spiritual being was doing a brilliant job of playing a baddie – very convincing, excellent performance.

From there I managed to move on to conjuring up the power of unconditional love. Two weeks later, completely out of the blue, I received a phone call from this person, spontaneously apologizing for everything she'd done. This was completely unsolicited, and totally out of character for her. I was stunned. I remember being speechless, but thrilled of course. Since that event, although I now have very few experiences with negative or mean people myself, I have helped others transform relationships using the power of unconditional love.

Margaret's Story *(A true story with names changed to protect privacy)*

I had been working with Margaret for a few months, and she had achieved impressive improvements in her energy levels. She was finding it easier to get up in the morning and wasn't fading in the afternoon as she had been before. However, something very dramatic had just happened and Margaret called me in a state. She had been called into her boss's office and told that there was a discrepancy in the accounts.

The bottom line is that Margaret had been accused of stealing from the company. She was horrified and devastated. She was also furious that anyone could believe that she was capable of stealing from anyone. In addition, she was furious that she had been accused before a proper investigation had been carried out.

Although Margaret could not get past the feelings of anger and horror in that moment, we went through the Beginner's Exercise and Superpower Exercise together until her state had changed enough for her to be able to fill herself with her power and maintain it. Then she sent the power to her boss, the company and the entire situation. Even if she was never proved innocent, even if they believed she was guilty, and even if she was fired because of it – she loved herself, the company, the people involved and the situation itself anyway.

I suggested that Margaret keep herself tuned in as much as possible, and resist the temptation to get into the emotion of the injustice of the issue. There is often a very powerful pull, in circumstances like this, to get into the feeling of the injustice and to soak in it. It's a human reaction and perfectly natural, but destructive. It is important to become aware of this and to pull away from it. Using the Beginner's Exercise and the Superpower Exercise helps.

As I explained to Margaret, when you feel yourself being pulled into that emotional quagmire of feelings of anger and injustice, it is like being stuck in a literal quagmire; and your superpower is the life line that can help you get out of it. If you stay in the emotion of injustice, you will be stuck there, and it will only create more of the same. Making the effort to resist the pull of that quagmire, grab the lifeline of your superpower and determine to hang on no matter what, will mean you get out of that state quickly, and the results are like magic.

Margaret had already seen significant results from using her superpower, and so she trusted it enough to resist the urge to dwell on the injustice, and instead kept going through the exercises to keep herself in the state of unconditional love. She made sure that she loved it all regardless of how it turned out.

It was only a couple of hours later that Margaret called me back, beside herself with excitement. She had just received a call from her boss at home, apologizing profusely and explaining there had been an error. Someone else had in fact made the error, and Margaret had done nothing wrong. Her boss went on to say that since Margaret's performance had been particularly impressive lately, she was putting her in charge of a new project.

The project was one Margaret had been desperate to get involved in, and she was ecstatic. It was also going to mean an opportunity for an increase in her bonus if she was able to make a success of this particular project.

If Margaret had allowed herself to get pulled into the feelings of injustice, she would probably have dwelled on how unfair the situation was, she would undoubtedly have confided in friends and colleagues about how badly she was being treated, and how dare her boss accuse her of stealing, and ... so on. Not only would the energy she was putting out have been entirely different, but her behavior, the way she spoke and the decisions she made would have been affected.

Instead, she shone light onto the darkness of false accusation, diffusing it. Where there may have been no way to prove her innocence, she didn't even have to – that was taken care of for her without her needing to even try. On top of that, her energy of unconditional love affected her boss on an unseen level, drawing attention to her value, and resulting in Margaret being given an opportunity she'd been wanting for a while but didn't think she would be given.

No matter how bad the situation or people are, your power will work. No matter how dark it is, your power will transform that darkness to light. But you have to switch it on.

When dealing with difficult or negative people: Choose to see the other person as a magnificent spiritual being who is playing the role of the "baddie" in your story - and appreciate their convincing performance!

Marriage and Other Romantic Relationships

There have been several instances of exes who transformed after being filled with the power of unconditional love. Here is one person's story (although "Jacky" is happy for her story to be told to inspire others, she asked for names to be changed).

Jacky's Story *(a true story with names changed for privacy)*

Jacky and Mike had been married for 12 years when they finally divorced. It was dramatic and traumatic for everyone involved, especially their son who was 7 years old at the time.

When Jacky first started writing to me she was frustrated, hurt and angry about not only the fact that Mike had left her for another woman, but also the way he was behaving throughout the process of the divorce. Mike seemed to not care that he had devastated the lives of his wife and son, and seemed to be focused only on his new life.

He was dragging his feet in the divorce proceedings, and barely made contact with his son. In her first email to me, Jacky explained that she couldn't see how she could ever even think about forgiving Mike, never mind feeling anything remotely related to unconditional love for him. The damage was just too deep, and his behavior beyond any reason.

It took some time for Jacky to begin to use her superpower on the situation. I guided her through developing the skill to fill just herself with it first. In circumstances like this, where there is a lot of hurt and anger, it is important to focus only on filling yourself with the power, without sending it anywhere.

In fact, while I'm here, I'll let you into a secret: the truth is: you don't actually need to send the love anywhere; you don't need to aim your superpower at what you want to change.

All you really need to do in order to see results in any area of your life and for any issue, is to fill yourself with that power, and maintain it; keep yourself topped up with it. That is the most important part of the process, and it works on its own. The reason we aim it at targets is for the benefit of the conscious mind.

The conscious mind can comprehend aiming and shooting the power at targets in order to affect them, just as you would with a magic wand or superhero power better than it can accept that simply keeping yourself full of that power will affect everything else in your life. So, we use the method of aiming and filling people, things and situations with the power since it does result in faster and more effective changes because the conscious mind is able to accept it more readily.

Back to Jacky. Because of the intense emotions Jacky was experiencing through this extremely challenging experience, not only was she unable at that point to send unconditional love to Mike; she was also unable to feel much of it for herself. In fact, she was "running on empty" as far as her superpower was concerned. Since you can't give what you don't have, it is essential that you only aim your power at targets once you are full of it yourself.

I suggested that Jacky focus solely on filling herself with her power using the Beginner's Exercise, and then move on to the Superpower Exercise, without the steps that involve allowing the power to overflow. I suggested she stop at the point where she is full of the power, and then practice maintaining that state for as long as possible.

Of course, at first, she found it difficult to tune in, but she was determined to create the changes she wanted in her life, and so she practiced consistently. She found that she was able to tune in easier each time she practiced, and her ability to maintain the state improved. She was able to hold the feeling of unconditional love for herself for longer and longer periods.

The next step I gave Jacky was to learn to tune in to her power using a power phrase. This enabled her to turn her power on instantly without needing to go through the exercises. With this new skill she was able to keep herself topped up with her power throughout her day, in the middle of any situation, regardless of where she was or what she was doing.

It had been about a week since Jacky first wrote to me, and she had been practicing using her power every day, several times a day as she wanted to master her skill to the point where she could use it to make changes as soon as possible. Towards the end of that week, she had already seen a few small changes in various areas of her life.

These ranged from feeling more energized, less stressed and happier than she had been before, to little coincidences and synchronicities. After that first week, Jacky was able to feel that she was full of her superpower most of the time, and it was now time to start practicing aiming it at targets.

I suggested she start with small things first, working her way up to the situation with Mike. She started with traffic and an unfriendly cashier in her bank, and found it really easy. There had been a few incidents involving Mike during that first week that had frustrated and angered her, including Mike forgetting to fetch their son from school.

Jacky had reacted with fury and bitterness at the time, but was able to later tune in and fill herself with her power. Now it was time to aim her superpower at him, and to fill him with the same unconditional love that filled her.

She tuned in to her power and filled herself with unconditional love; then she imagined her power overflowing from her and filling the room she was in. Next, she thought of Mike, and imagined the power filling him, from his toes up to the top of his head. She found it much easier than she expected.

She imagined him at his worst and imagined that he would never change, and kept that power filling him. She was able to think of all of the things he had done, and keep that power filling him; loving him anyway. She made sure that she felt the feeling of loving him anyway, even if he never changed.

Jacky wrote to me later to say that she couldn't get over how much easier it was than she expected. The next step was to use her power whenever Mike said or did anything that upset or annoyed her. Right in the middle of whatever it was, she was to tune in to her power, feel it filing herself and then see it filling him. Jacky managed to achieve this a couple of times, but there were one or two occasions when she just couldn't do it.

When she wrote to me for advice on these instances I suggested that she simply tune in whenever she can, after the incident, and then love the fact that she couldn't tune in. Love the fact that she couldn't feel love. More about that powerful technique later.

A few days later, she received a phone call from Mike who was friendlier than usual; he sounded very upbeat and in good spirits. He told her that he was about to leave town for a week, and that he had signed the paperwork the lawyer was waiting for and would drop it off at the lawyer's office the next morning. He also asked if he could take their son on a day out. It was Thursday when he called; he would be leaving town on the Monday and wanted to take their son to a theme park on the Saturday.

Although Jacky was pleasantly surprised she said she was skeptical because of his previous broken promises. So, she didn't tell her son about the trip, and decided it would be a surprise if Mike did turn up; and if he didn't, she will have spared her son the disappointment.

She received a call from the lawyer on Friday afternoon to say he had received the signed paperwork from Mike. On Saturday, Jacky waited for Mike to arrive to fetch their son. He had promised to be there at 9am. It was now 10.15am, and Jacky was seething. She was glad she hadn't told their son about the outing.

Then she remembered to use her superpower. She took a moment to try to feel her power, but found it difficult; so she went back to the Beginner's Exercise to get herself tuned in, and that worked instantly. Jacky filled herself with her power first, and then aimed it at Mike. She imagined that he had completely forgotten their son, and kept him full of the power anyway. She imagined that he didn't care about her or their son, and was too busy with his new romance to remember their son was waiting for him, and she loved him anyway.

At 10.30am, Mike called to say he was delayed, but would be there in 15 minutes. He didn't say why he was delayed, and Jacky felt her relief mixed with anger. She went through the exercise again and made sure that she was filling Mike with her superpower even if he didn't have a good reason for being late, and even if he still didn't actually turn up at all (just in case!).

Mike arrived at 10.50am, apologized briefly without an explanation, but was friendly and warm – a side to him she hadn't seen for a long time. Their son was ecstatic when his father turned up unexpectedly and told him they were going to the theme park.

The relationship between Jacky and Mike is not perfect, and there are still things that Jacky finds difficult to accept; but the stress, drama, hurt, anger and frustration are no longer a part of the relationship. They even have a laugh together occasionally. It is certainly a complete transformation from where it was. Jacky has gone on to use her superpower for many other aspects of her life, and is now dating a man with whom she has a lot of fun, and who gets on well with her son.

Isabelle's Story *(names changed to protect privacy)*

Isabelle had been single for some time when she sent me a message on a forum asking whether the superpower could work for finding a boyfriend. I suggested she start by using the Superpower Exercise to fill herself with the power first of course, and then I recommended she make a list of everything she wanted in a boyfriend – the qualities that were most important to her.

The next step was to use the Superpower Exercise to tune in, and then fill that list with the power; loving those qualities even if she never found anyone with them. She was to imagine that she would never find a boyfriend, and aim her power at that outcome, like shining a light into darkness. I asked her to check that she was fully tuned in to her power by making sure that she felt love for herself even if she was never going to find a boyfriend, as well as for any other "worst case scenario" she thought of.

In addition to this, I suggested Isabelle follow what feels good in the moment, every moment. We are often led to what we want in the most unlikely ways. Over the next couple of weeks, Isabelle wrote to me a couple of times, feeling despondent. She had been out on a couple of dates, but the guys she was meeting were nothing like the man she imagined being with. I reminded Isabelle that she was still developing her skill, and that it was crucial to keep going.

Just like learning any new skill, it's important to keep practicing until you get the results you want; and consider any delays or setbacks as just part of the process of improving. In addition, I advised that Isabelle not deliberately go out to try to meet guys, but instead, to simply follow what feels good instead of what seems logical.

Isabelle persevered, and began turning down social invitations when she didn't feel like going. Previously she was accepting all invitations whether she felt like going or not, assuming that she would never find her man otherwise. One of these occasions involved the birthday party of a friend of a friend.

Isabelle didn't know the birthday girl very well, having only met her a few times; but she'd agreed to go to the party when her friend, Stacey pointed out that there would be lots of guys she hadn't met before, and maybe she would meet her dream man that night.

However, the day before the party, her sister called her to say she had tickets for a show she had been wanting to see. Isabelle later said that although she chose to see the show with her sister because that felt better, there was a small part of her that believed she should have gone to the party as she might be missing meeting the man of her dreams there.

As it happens, at the theater, they bumped into an old friend of Isabelle's sister's who invited them both to join her and a group of friends for a drink after the show.

Isabelle had thought at the time that she might pop in to the birthday party after the show, but it felt better to stay with her sister and go for a drink with the group. One of the guys in the group was a scuba diving teacher. He and Isabelle got chatting; and when she mentioned she'd always wanted to try scuba diving, he invited her to attend one of the training sessions at the public swimming pool.

To cut a long story short, it was at one of the diving classes that Isabelle met her current boyfriend. By that time she had forgotten about the list she'd made of the qualities she wanted in a boyfriend. She remembered it some time later, dug it out, and realized that she is with a man who has all of the qualities on her list.

By practicing using her superpower, and by following what felt good instead of what made sense, Isabelle was led to her dream man. All along, I encouraged Isabelle to use her superpower to love the outcome no matter what it may be; to keep herself topped up with unconditional love regardless of what may happen. And although she struggled at times, she kept practicing until it got easier.

You can use your superpower for any kind of relationship from those with family and friends to spouses and partners, to clients, bosses, work colleagues and strangers. It works from any distance; and it works even if you've never met the person. The most important thing to remember is that in order for it to work, you need to make sure that you are completely filled with your power yourself before you aim it at anyone else.

I'll share with you, later in this book, exercises you can use to develop your ability, and the process for using your power to transform your relationships with others.

Fill yourself with unconditional love, regardless of what the outcome may be. That is the core of your power; and that is how you will create the experiences you want.

What About Free Will?

Of course, one of the most common questions regarding the subject of changing other people's behavior using this power is the question of free will. How can we make someone else change their behavior or attitude without their cooperation? The truth is: we can't. No-one can make someone else change against their will. What you are changing with this power is your experience of the other person, not necessarily the other person themselves.

If that person is open to change; if they are open to it even just on a subconscious level, they may well change within themselves. However, if they are not open to change at all, since it is your experience of that person that you are changing, circumstances will adjust accordingly. Perhaps you will simply happen to not be around them when they are in that state or mood; or something may occur that results in their leaving your experience altogether – they may be transferred or get another job, or you may receive a new promotion or job offer.

As long as you are tuned in to your power, have filled yourself with it first, and then aimed it at that person, your experience of that person will change in one way or another. It is important to remember that in order for this to work you need to be fully tuned in to your power; and in order to remain fully tuned in, you need to be feeling unconditional love.

That means that you fill the other person with love even if they never change, even if the entire situation remains exactly as it is. Remember, the power is in the *unconditional*. When you love something exactly as it is, you release it; you let go of whatever is holding it in your experience.

When you use your superpower on other people, it is your experience of that person you are changing.

How Unconditional Love Works in the Work Place

Your superpower can be used to change work circumstances and conditions; it can be used for promotions, and recognition as well as success in meetings and interviews. It can even be used to manifest your dream job.

I recently worked with a client who desperately wanted a specific job. The job she was in wasn't what she really wanted to do. She used the techniques in this book to aim her power at the job she was in at the time, and at the job she wanted. She ended up in her dream job, at very close to the salary she had desired. She was over the moon, and stunned that it had worked. I'll share her story with you in detail later in this chapter.

I use my power to pre-pave meetings, gigs, phone calls, speaking engagements, and anything else to do with my work. Before I leave home, or before I arrive at the venue, I go through the Superpower exercise, which I will share with you later in this book, and I saturate the room I'm going to be in, and all the people who will be there, in unconditional love.

This means I fill myself, the room, and everyone there with love regardless of how it will turn out. Whether the event goes well or not, whether the people like me or not, I love them. And I have not had one bad experience since I started doing this.

There have been times – especially in the beginning – when I forgot to pre-pave. I can remember a couple of examples right now. I would be in the middle of the event, and it wasn't going very well at all. In those incidents, I immediately – right there, in the middle of the event – used my power to fill myself, the room, and everyone in it with unconditional love... and every single time, things turned around!

People warmed to me, and ended up loving me; attendance increased, rain stopped, people turned up who had not been planning on coming, people agreed to things they had been arguing against. Every time, the conditions of the event transformed.

When you have a meeting, interview, or presentation, spend a few minutes using the Superpower exercise some time before you go in, and make sure you fill yourself first. As I explain in the exercise, you can't give what you don't have, so it's important to always make sure you're topped up with unconditional love for yourself first, and then let it overflow to your target. The Superpower exercise will help you do this.

You'll be amazed at the results this pre-paving produces, and you'll be stunned at the magic that happens when you use your power in the middle of unwanted circumstances. In a situation where you're feeling worried, nervous, shy or intimidated, this will turn everything around for you. Your superpower is an excellent antidote for nervousness, shyness and fear.

Getting into a state of unconditional love before going in to work, into a meeting or for an interview, will fill you with your power. This will, of course raise your energy; affect your posture, your presence, body language, tone of voice, the things you say, and your expressions. And it will all be natural – an automatic result of the state you're in. You will feel calm and in control, and you will give the impression to others of being confident and competent.

Use your superpower with clients and customers. Getting into the state of unconditional love before you see a client or customer will directly affect the results you achieve. You'll find that your superpower is also extremely effective on colleagues and bosses. If the person you work for or with is difficult, unappreciative or even downright rude, try using this power on them.

It may seem impossible at first, but as you practice the exercises, you'll find it gets easier and easier. You will be able to fill yourself with the power first, using the Beginner's Exercise and the Superpower Exercise, and then you will be able to aim it at that person just as you would shine a torch into darkness. No matter what your situation at work, you will be able to transform it using this power.

Here are a few examples of how the superpower works on relationships with people at work.

Andrew's Story

Andrew loves his job, but his enjoyment is marred by the fact that he shares an office with one of the most miserable people he's ever met. Jack complains constantly. He seems to do this on automatic. Every day, going in to the office, Andrew dreads seeing Jack; each morning, Jack goes into great detail on what is wrong with the company they work for, their clients, and the world at large. He even gives Andrew a rundown of why he (Andrew) will never get any further in his career. No matter how positive Andrew is, Jack's diatribe is sure to knock him down.

Andrew decides to use his superpower on Jack and the entire situation; so he creates a routine of using the Superpower Exercise every morning before going to work. After filling himself with his power, he aims it at the whole office, and then Jack in particular. At first, it is difficult to aim the power at Jack, to feel love for him even if he never changes. But, with practice, Andrew is able to achieve this. For a week, he goes through the exercise every morning; and whenever he thinks of it throughout the day while he is at work, he tunes in to his power and aims it at Jack - especially while Jack is complaining.

Nothing happens, and Andrew feels a little despondent. The thought "It's not working" pops into his head more than once. Then he reminds himself that this is a skill he is developing; and although the power itself seems to be magical, he still has to develop the skill to use it.

If he was learning to play an instrument, and after a week of practicing just a few minutes a day he was unable to play his favorite song, he wouldn't come to the conclusion that the instrument "isn't working", he would realize that he simply needs more practice. And so, he decides to keep going, keep practicing.

Reminding himself that he is developing a skill helps a lot. It means the more he practices, the more proficient he will get, and the faster and more impressive the results will be. He starts to see it as the difference between playing a CD and playing an instrument.

With the CD he would only need to place it into a CD player and press "Play" to hear the songs that have been recorded; with an instrument, he would need to learn how to play it, to master the instrument in order to get what he wants out of it. So, Andrew continues to practice the Superpower exercise every morning before going to work, and he continues to do his best to tune in to his power while he is at work, being sure to fill himself with it first, and then aiming it at Jack.

A couple of days later, Andrew arrives at the office to find Jack in a more agitated state than usual. Jack's topic of complaint this morning is *the fact that he has just received notice that he is being transferred to a different department.*

In this case, Jack didn't change, but Andrew's experience of him did. Depending on whether the other person is subconsciously or energetically open to change or not, their behavior may change or circumstances will change. Either way, if you use your superpower on other people, whether they are willing to change their behavior or not, your experience of them will certainly change.

Sarah's Story *(Based on a true story with names and setting changed)*

Sarah has been working in retail for 4 years, but has only been working at the new store for around 3 months. She enjoys working in the busy store, and the rest of the staff members have been very welcoming and friendly. Except for one. One of the other sales assistants, Becca, seems to have an issue with Sarah, and Sarah has no idea what it could be. She barely knows Becca, yet Becca is blatantly rude to her.

Sarah, a naturally friendly person, smiles at Becca and greets her, just as she does the others; Becca makes eye contact with Sarah, with no smile at all, and turns her head away, shunning her. Sarah notices that Becca is friendly with everyone else, and seems like a genuinely nice person, so Sarah feels hurt and indignant that she is so dismissive and rude to just her. Her brain can't seem to stop mulling over it and trying to figure out what she's done to deserve that kind of treatment.

Sarah decides to use her superpower. It's difficult because she feels that Becca is in the wrong, and her natural instinct is to treat Becca in the same way Becca is treating her. She wants to ignore her – give her "a bit of her own medicine." But, she realizes that choosing to treat Becca in that way would be compromising her own personality, and it certainly wouldn't do anything to improve the situation.

So, in order to be able to use her superpower with Becca, she chooses to see Becca's rudeness as darkness, and her own friendliness and warmth, along with her superpower, as light. She will shine the light into Becca's darkness; and since darkness cannot survive in light, but a light can shine in the dark, her light will cause the darkness to either transform to light, or leave her experience in some other way.

Sarah spends a little time each morning before going in to work, going through the Superpower Exercise, filling herself with the power first, and then seeing it fill the entire store, and in particular, Becca. She sees Becca being filled with the power from her toes all the way up to the top of her head, and she makes sure the love is unconditional. She loves Becca exactly as she is, even if she never changes.

In fact, Sarah imagines Becca snubbing her again, and keeps that power going, filling Becca even as she snubs Sarah and walks away. In addition to practicing the Superpower Exercise every morning before work, Sarah also makes sure she is topped up with her superpower before she enters the store, and when she sees Becca, she is just as warm and friendly as she is to everyone else. When Becca snubs her on the first day, she keeps that power going, and sees Becca being filled with it.

It only takes two days before Sarah sees a change. She arrives for work, two days after starting to use her superpower on Becca, and greets Becca with her usual warmth. She is stunned to see Becca smile warmly back at her and cheerily say "Hi, Sarah" and continue tidying the shelves.

Sarah takes a moment to absorb what has just happened, and feels a thrill at the power of what she has just achieved. From then on, Becca treats Sarah as she does everyone else. She is warm and friendly, with no sign of her earlier surliness. Sarah resists the temptation to try to make sense of it; to try to work out why Becca treated her that way in the first place, and simply enjoys the results, and in particular the potency of her superpower.

Sarah's story is a real experience; and although the names and setting have been changed to protect Becca's identity, everything else is true. Sarah's and Becca's personalities, the circumstances between them, and the remarkable change in Becca are all related exactly as they happened.

Here is an example of how your superpower can be used to change the circumstances of your job. This story is a true experience, related exactly as it happened. Snigdha is a coaching client of mine who has achieved remarkable results using the power of unconditional love, and she has generously agreed to share her experience with others. This is her experience in her own words.

Snigdha's Story *(A true story)*

"The job where I was at before was satisfactory but not what I wanted. However I was grateful because it paid the bills and I had made good friends with my co-workers. Though I had used UL (unconditional love) to exponentially make the atmosphere MUUUUCH better than before, it wasn't where I wanted to be. Also I had just stumbled upon UL 3 weeks before and was still trying to test it out.

So in April 2014 my boss called me into his office and told me that they'd be laying me off at the end of this month because the firm wasn't doing so well etc. My boss told me I was doing good work but they simply couldn't afford to keep me. I understood and thanked him for all the experience I got etc.

After that meeting I was really stressed and upset. It was one thing to decide within myself that I wanted to change jobs, quite another to have an ultimatum handed to me. Anyways, I decided that this is the perfect opportunity to use UL. I sat down at my PC to work and was going through my mail when I saw an email from the company where I work now, saying that my CV had been shortlisted for an online test.

I thought it was a hoax at first, like one of those emails where they ask for your personal details etc. to steal from you so, I didn't put too much into it. Curious, I searched the company's name, profile etc. and it all came up clean. By NOW I was over excited. I couldn't sit STILL! My colleagues at work thought I was having an upset stomach or something :p I wanted to jump up and down and went to the bathroom and did just that! :P Lol I was BLOWN AWAY that UL worked so fast and so ...miraculously!!

So I gave the first online test, and cleared it. I had to wait another week to hear back and throughout that week I gave UL to it. I, of course, felt anxious, but whenever I DID, I gave UL and used Odille's advice about loving the job EVEN if I DIDNT get it. It was REALLLLY hard at first :P I mean but I kind of got to a place where I felt like ok, I can do this, even if I DONT get this, something better WILL be given. I mean all that UL couldn't have just gone to waste!

SO next week I got an email saying that I was selected for the final round of interviews which would be conducted over the phone. And yes, I cleared the final round as well, it went marvelously, the CEO loved me and we negotiated and settled on a neat little package. My salary was VERRRRY close to what I wanted and very satisfying!

And soooo, I feel happy just thinking about it, I got a new job, where I get to work from home (woohoo!), flexible working hours, a great salary boost, AND the best part, I get to do what I love. Of course NOW that I know how it all works, I'm going to be using it to get an even better job, but this example has given me a sort of confidence that I never had before. Now I KNOW that no matter what life throws at me, I just whip out my UL wand like in Harry Potter and it's all good! :D Actually no, it's all fabulous. And ALL thanks to Odille! I love her and owe her all the amazing changes in my life! She's a shining star and is always there to help guide me!

Thank you!!" - *Snigdha Jain, Delhi*

As you can see from these examples, your superpower can be used to achieve changes that seem unlikely, or even impossible. The more you practice, the easier it gets, and the better you get at using your power.

The most important things to remember are:

- You are developing a skill, and that takes practice. Although it can work very quickly, if you find it is taking some time, remind yourself that just like any skill, mastering your superpower takes practice.
- Think of the thing you don't want (whether it is a person's behavior, a circumstance, or any other aspect of your work life) as darkness; and your superpower as your torch. No matter how bad the target seems to you, aiming your superpower at it (shining your torch into the darkness) is the most effective way to transform it.
- It is your experience you are changing, not necessarily other people. Although you may find, as was the case with Becca, the behavior of the other person changes, that will depend on whether they are subconsciously open to changing or not. But, whether they change in themselves, or not, your experience of them will change (as was the case in Andrew's story).

Choose to see the things you don't want as darkness; aiming unconditional love at those things is like shining light into darkness. It will release the darkness and transform it to light.

How Unconditional Love Works With Finances

Everything in this universe is vibrating. And everything we experience in our lives is a result of how we're vibrating. We attract and create only whatever is a vibrational match – whatever is vibrating on the same frequency as we are. This means that you cannot attract or create abundance while you're vibrating lack. And, luckily, you also cannot attract lack while you're vibrating abundance. So, if you don't have the money you want, you must be vibrating at a different frequency to it.

Now, this may seem unlikely. For a long time, I couldn't understand why I was experiencing such financial struggle when I was certain I didn't have a "poverty mentality". I had changed my views on money years before, and I knew that I now believed that money is good and plentiful, and that resources expand as demand grows.

I strongly believed that there's enough for everyone, and my having money would not take away from anyone else... and so on. I certainly didn't believe money was evil. I had examined my beliefs, and I was absolutely sure that I had not one negative belief about money. And yet, I was still struggling to pay the bills. What more could I do?

It was my sister who pointed out to me that I had low self-esteem. I laughed. I'm an actress and singer, how on earth could I have low self-esteem? I had spent my life believing I had high self-esteem and confidence. My sister said "Think about it. If you had high self-esteem, why would you be creating lack and struggle?" That made me think. It made me think deeply. She had an excellent point. I already believed that we all create and attract all experiences in our lives, so why would I be creating financial struggle?

As I dug around in my beliefs, I discovered that although I was confident when I performed, I did, in fact have very low self-esteem. I had feelings of inferiority and unworthiness and lack. Suddenly, the financial issues made sense.

I decided to go on a mission to learn to love myself. I tried various methods – all of which I found uncomfortable. And then, something hit me. We don't have to love ourselves! We already do! We're born with love for ourselves, but it's conditioned out of us. We learn, through being taught and through our life experience, that it is bad to love yourself. We're taught to put others first, not to show off, not to get "too big for your boots", not to brag.

Self-love is confused with conceit and arrogance. And so, we learn to suppress our love for ourselves, and reprogram ourselves with self-deprecation, self-criticism and judgment. We learn to criticize and judge ourselves the way others criticize and judge us. We learn that when we are harder on ourselves than others are, we get more approval. And so, the love we have for ourselves is blocked out.

What I discovered is, instead of trying to love myself, all I had to do was recognize that I already do. I started deliberately looking around me for evidence of the love I have for myself. Since we create and attract everything in our lives, that means that every good thing that happens to me, every good thing that has ever happened to me, is an expression of love from myself, to myself.

I started noticing it was sunny, and saying, "Look how much I love myself!" I would notice that the traffic light turned green as I approached the intersection, and say, "Look how much I love myself"; I would notice the smile from a stranger, and say, "Look how much I love myself". Before I knew it, I was feeling intense, genuine, glorious – and most importantly, natural - love for myself! Since that time, I have never been back into that financial struggle.

The full explanation of this method of developing self-love is detailed in the books **THE MAGIC PILL** and **THE SECOND DOSE**, as well as **BEYOND THE MAGIC PILL**.

So, the first step to transforming your financial situation (and all other areas of your life) is to start recognizing and acknowledging the fact that you love yourself. And as you do, as you say to yourself with each one "Look how much I love myself!" you will feel the amazing energy of your power; and the more you do it, the stronger it will become.

When you receive a bill that you cannot pay, it would be natural for you to feel upset, anxious, maybe frustrated. But, bearing in mind the frequency at which you're vibrating attracts more of the same, and bearing in mind how you feel is how you're vibrating, and also considering the experiments mentioned in an earlier chapter which prove that how we feel directly affects the world around us, it would make more sense to find a way to not feel those negative feelings.

By doing whatever it takes to find a way to feel good will mean you won't be attracting more reasons to feel upset, anxious and frustrated, and maybe even more bills you can't pay. In fact, it would be ideal if you could immediately get out of that negative state and change it to a feeling of abundance and joy so that you would be then attracting more reasons to feel abundance and joy. You would be attracting more abundance and fewer bills. If only there were a switch you could flick …
Wait a minute, there is! ☺

Through developing your ability to use your superpower, you will be able to look at a bill you cannot pay, and conjure a feeling of unconditional love. This is the same frequency as abundance and joy. And as you switch, in that moment, from despair to unconditional love, you will be matching up with abundance. And as you continue to use your power, you will begin to spend more time feeling good than you do feeling bad. And it's how you feel MOST of the time that determines what you're creating and attracting.

A few months ago I did a job for a company that I had worked with once before. The last time I worked with them, which was seven years ago, they were extremely slow to pay. I had to chase them for months before they finally paid me. So, when they offered me a job again this year, I was initially hesitant to take it because of that previous experience with them. However, I chose to take the job and use the power of unconditional love on the situation instead of either turning it down or doing the job with apprehension regarding payment.

Before I accepted the job I tuned in to my power, filled myself with unconditional love and then sent it to the company, everyone involved, and the job itself. In addition to that, during the job I continued to keep myself topped up with unconditional love, as well as filling the company, the people and the job with it.

I kept the whole situation filled with love, regardless of whether they were slow to pay me or not. In fact, I loved them all even if they never paid me. I also made sure I was in this state when I emailed the invoice to them after I had completed the job. "Even if they take months to pay me and I have to chase them; even if they never pay me, I love them anyway." The money was in my bank account by the next evening.

The skill comes in mastering the following conundrum: Even though you are using this power to achieve the result you want, you need to let go of that idea in order to successfully use the power. In other words, the reason I was using the power of unconditional love in this situation was because I wanted to be paid promptly of course; but while I was using the power, I made sure that I genuinely felt love for the situation and all involved even if I never got paid.

It sounds impossible at first, and it is something that took me a while to fully grasp and understand; but I can assure you that the more you practice the technique, the easier it gets. And although I can remember the contradiction from when I first started practicing using this power, it is no longer a contradiction for me.

It is now perfectly acceptable and extremely easy to use this power in order to achieve a result while feeling genuine love for the alternative outcome. This is because the power is not an emotion. It is an energy; and with practice you will develop the ability to separate that power, that energy, from your emotions and thoughts.

Here is another experience from my own life that demonstrates the power of unconditional love with money.

I was invited to a convention in Las Vegas, USA (I live in the United Kingdom) however, although attendance to the conference was free, I would have to pay for my own airfare and expenses. At the time, I had very little money, and could see no way of getting enough to pay for such a trip. This was March, and the convention was taking place in June.

I decided that if I was going to attend, I wanted to take my partner and son with me. Since it was a long way to go, and I have family who live there, who I hadn't seen for several years, I wanted to add a week's vacation to the five day convention, increasing the trip to two weeks. I decided all of this even though I could see no way of getting the money to pay for even just my airfare, never mind three return airfares and expenses for two weeks.

I worked out how much the entire trip would cost, comfortably. Apart from the airfares, I included accommodation, spending money, and the cost of several experiences including: a visit to Bonnie Springs cowboy town attraction, where we would stay overnight in the motel, followed by a breakfast horse-back ride through Red Rock Canyon the next morning; attending the "Tournament of Kings" jousting show and dinner at the Excalibur Hotel (both my son and my partner were very into medieval England, knights, sword-fighting and jousting – this show was an enormously fun experience for them in particular!); and indoor skydiving, amongst many other fun activities and sight-seeing.

I worked out that the trip would cost £2,000 in total, for all three of us to enjoy all of those experiences and to have plenty of spending money to make the trip comfortable.

We talked about it every morning on the school run, and reveled in the excitement. We planned all of the activities and knew that we were going, even though at that point there was no sign of the money. I also spent time filling myself and the whole trip with unconditional love (I hadn't yet created the Superpower Exercise). I imagined that we would never get the money in time, and that we would not be able to go, and I filled that option with love as well. I loved it all anyway, even if we never went to Vegas.

At the beginning of April I received a call from a recording studio for which I had auditioned the previous year. The audition had been for a voice-over job - to play the narrator of the UK version of the animated television series "Hello Kitty"; and the recording had been scheduled for

February. When I hadn't heard anything from them by the end of February I knew I hadn't got the job (they generally only contact you if you get it; so, if you don't hear anything, you know that you didn't get the job). The call I received in April was to tell me I had been chosen as the narrator, and the schedule had been delayed to April and May (which is why I hadn't heard before). There were 26 episodes to record, and it was paying.... £2,000.

Needless to say, the three of us went to Las Vegas in June, enjoyed a magical vacation, doing all of the activities we had planned, spent precious time with family, and came home with our heads full of wonderful memories, and a fabulous video of our family indoor skydiving session.

The reason I am sharing this particular experience with you is to illustrate how, even though you may not be able to see any possibility of reaching your desire right now; even though it seems impossible, there will be a way. Using unconditional love helps to release resistance and doubt, which in turn allows the circumstances and people into your experience that will lead you to your desire. One of the most significant effects of your superpower is dissolving resistance.

You don't need to learn to love yourself; you already do. All you need to do is start recognizing that you already love yourself by noticing and acknowledging every good thing in your life as an expression of love from yourself, to yourself.

How Unconditional Love Works with The Law of Attraction

You may have heard Abraham speak (Abraham-Hicks – reference at the back of this book). They are, in my opinion, the top authority on the Law of Attraction. The basic, and most important points of what they teach are:

1. **We are all vibrational beings focused in a physical experience.**
2. **How we vibrate attracts and creates stuff (for want of a better word ☺) that vibrates at the same frequency.**
3. **How we feel is an indication of how we are vibrating.**
4. **There is nothing more important than feeling good because while you are feeling good, you have no resistance to all of the "stuff" you've asked for.**

They came up with an analogy a few years ago which helps to clarify what we need to do in order to attract everything we want; from relationships to health, to finances, to events, to material goods, and everything else. They described the frequency of all the "good stuff" we've asked for as a Vortex. A vibrational vortex.

They explained that if you imagine that everything you've ever wanted is in this vortex – which is vibrating at a specific frequency, in order to get your stuff, you need to get into the vortex where the stuff is. In order to manifest everything you want, you need to join it on the same frequency.

They give various processes you can use to "get into your vortex". They describe how what you focus on affects how you feel, which determines the frequency at which you are vibrating. And so, if you change your focus, you'll change how you feel, which will automatically change the frequency.

Unconditional love will take you directly into the vortex – instantly and without the need for a thought process. You'll be able to get into the vortex – and stay there – no matter what is going on around you. Right in the middle of drama, negativity, arguments, upset, frustration, worry... right in the middle of whatever is going on, you will be able to instantly get into the vortex! And you will be able to stay there for longer periods of time, which will enable all of the stuff you've asked for, to manifest.

Another great analogy Abraham use is the High-Flying Disk. They explain that if you get into a state of joy and appreciation, this raises your vibration – the equivalent of being on a high-flying disk. And as long as you are on that disk (in that state of joy and appreciation) it is not possible for you to rendezvous with anything or anyone else who is not on that same disk (matching that same state). And so, they encourage you to get onto that disk when you wake in the morning, and try and stay on it for as long as you can.

When you are channeling the power of unconditional love, you are automatically on that disk, and it will keep you there. It will keep you in that state for longer than anything else can. You don't have to avoid negativity or bad thoughts – using your superpower will transform them. We can't always avoid negative situations.

Sometimes we're stuck in a car with someone who is detailing all the bad stuff going on in their world, or a client we can't avoid is sharing with us, the latest tragedy on the news. Your superpower will enable you to, right in the middle of that - while that person is still going on about the terrible state of affairs - jump onto that high-flying disk, and stay there. And miraculously, you'll notice the negativity cannot be sustained as long as you're on your high-flying disk.

Something will happen to end it. Either the person will be distracted, or one of you will get a phone call or be called away, or... there are infinite possibilities. No matter what happens, you will be able to sustain your feeling of bliss regardless of what is going on around you. And as long as you stay in that state, you cannot rendezvous with anything that is not on the same disk.

In addition to all of this, unconditional love is the ultimate way to release resistance. When you want to create or attract something in your life, and you've visualized it, and you have the feeling of it, often the thought of the lack or absence of it will create resistance and therefore block the manifestation.

This is because of course, the frequency of the lack of what you want is different to the frequency of having what you want. And many of us find it difficult to keep our thoughts from wandering over to notice that what we want hasn't turned up yet. In order to allow your manifestation, you need to release and let go, and allow the Universe to do its thing, without checking up on it. Each time you notice your desire hasn't manifested, you're delaying its arrival. It's like digging up a seed to check if it's growing yet.

Here's the solution: Using your superpower - loving the lack, loving yourself and the entire situation even if it never happens - releases the resistance. I know it sounds wrong at first, and it's quite a contradiction, but trust me, it's the way your power works. And it works like magic!

So, let's say you want to manifest a new car, here's the process you would use: You'd conjure up your power using the Superpower Exercise to fill yourself with unconditional love for yourself first (you can't give it unless you're full of it yourself), you would then have your power overflow from you, to fill the room you're in. Then you would send it to the car you want.

You'd imagine seeing the car, and see your power filling the car, overflowing from the car and filling the dealership or the lot, or the garage – wherever it might be. You don't need to know where the car is, just pick a place and use that for the exercise. Then see everyone (meaning anyone who might be there – again, you don't need to know who they are) being filled up with your power as well.

Next… and this step is the tricky bit, but it's where the potency of your power lies – it's the bit that makes it work. Imagine never getting that car. Imagine you'll never have that car, or in fact any new car. And love it anyway! This may seem impossible at first, but trust me, it only takes practice and it gets easier and easier – and this step is vital for the power to work effectively. See that power, and feel that unconditional love filling yourself, the car, the location of the car and all who are there. Love it all anyway even if you never get it.

When you manage to do this, you will feel the most liberating joy. It's immensely freeing to be able to love what you don't want. And that is what will get you what you do want. As I said, it's an odd contradiction, and if I hadn't mastered it myself I wouldn't believe it was possible. But I live like this now. I use this every day. Loving what you don't want is your power. Remember, your power of unconditional love is your torch, and when you shine it into the darkness of what you don't want, or what you fear, or what you worry about, it transforms the darkness to light.

The lack of what you want, not getting what you want, is the darkness; and as long as you fear that, it will stay with you and it will stay dark. And it won't allow in the thing you want. When you love that lack, when you love the fact that you don't have what you want, you are releasing it, you are shining a light on the darkness. That releases it and transforms it into light, allowing in what you want.

It may seem, at times, that it's not "working" when you are not seeing the results. Here is an analogy that explains what is happening:

The lack of the new car is darkness. The fact that you don't have the car is darkness. Unconditional love is light. Loving the fact that you don't have the new car is shining light into the darkness. Now, it takes time for the darkness to transform into light (since we are living in a time-space reality).

When you stop loving the fact that you don't have the new car, and you worry that it is not coming, or you feel frustrated that this "isn't working" you have switched off the light; you have switched off your torch, and the darkness returns. In fact, the edges of the darkness that had begun to transform into light, reform into darkness again.

You may not be able to see how your car is coming to you, but that does not mean that "nothing's happening". As long as you are following what feels good in the moment, every moment, you are being led to your goal. Here is an example of how synchronicity works when you are following what feels good in the moment, every moment:

Alison wants a new second-hand car, but doesn't have a budget for a decent one. She would really like a Ford Fiesta 1.25 Zetec 5dr. Ideally she'd like a light blue one; but as long as it is in good condition she's not too concerned about the color. She searches the ads in the newspaper and online listings, but there are no Ford Fiesta 1.25 Zetecs available for the price she can afford. So, she spends some time thinking about the car, imagining what it is like to drive it, and she fills herself and the car with the energy of unconditional love. Then she imagines that she will never get that car.

Because she has been practicing the Superpower Exercise, she has developed the skill of feeling love for the outcome she doesn't want; so she imagines she will never have the car she wants, and then she loves it anyway. She loves herself anyway, loves the car anyway – wherever it may end up, and loves the fact that she will never have it.

Then she chooses to follow what feels good in the moment, every moment; even if it has nothing to do with getting the car. She knows that following what feels good in the moment is the treasure hunt trail to what she wants. One Saturday afternoon, a friend, Shanti asks Alison to go bowling with her and a few other friends.

Alison has just found an ad for an old Honda Civic that is within her price range and has arranged to view it later that afternoon. The car is in a town about an hour's drive away. It's not the car she wants, but it's very cheap and she's almost given up on the Fiesta.

However, since she has made the decision to follow what feels good in the moment she decides to weigh up which option feels good in this moment. She imagines going to look at the Civic. It doesn't feel so good to drive an hour to look at a car that is cheap but not the one she wants, and miss a great outing with good friends. Part of her feels she should go though, since she really needs a car as her old one is practically falling apart.

Then she imagines what it would feel like to choose to go bowling with Shanti instead of driving to look at the Civic, and that feels so much better. It really feels fun. For a moment she is torn – part of her believes she should go and check out the car since it is really cheap and seems in excellent condition; and she's unlikely to get another opportunity for such a good deal. On the other hand, if she were to follow what feels good in the moment, she would forget the car and go bowling with her friends.

So, since she has decided to follow what feels good, she uses the Superpower exercise to fill herself with unconditional love and then sends it to the car she wants (loving it even if she never gets it), then she sends it to the Civic and to the fact that she won't be going to see it. Even if it turns out she has made the wrong choice and she never finds a car she can afford, she loves the whole situation anyway.

Alison calls Shanti back and tells her she'd love to go bowling. Shanti offers Alison a lift, and fetches her at 2pm. On the way to the bowling alley, Shanti pulls over to a gas station to fill up with fuel. When she goes in to pay, she asks Alison if she wants anything. Alison decides she would like a candy bar and it feels good to go into the gas station with Shanti.

They enter the store and while Shanti is paying for the fuel, Alison remembers she doesn't have the latest copy of her favorite magazine; so she goes over to where the magazines are displayed to look for it.

While she is looking for the magazine, she sees a notice board right next to the magazine rack. Shanti is now waiting to leave the store, but it feels good to Alison to have a look at the ads on the notice board, so she asks Shanti if she would mind waiting. Shanti is happy to wait, and looks through the magazines.

Alison sees an ad on the notice board that reads: "Used 2004 VW Golf for sale. Good condition. $4,000". There is a photo of the car, she can see it looks in good condition, and it's a light blue color. She takes down the number. It's not a Fiesta, and the price is higher than the Civic, but she'll have a look at it. She tunes in to her superpower right there in the store; fills herself with unconditional love, sends it to the Fiesta she wants even if she never gets it, and sends it to the Golf even if she doesn't get it. As Alison and Shanti walk back to Shanti's car, a pale blue Ford Fiesta pulls into the gas station.

Alison feels a thrill at the coincidence of seeing the car she wants right after thinking about it. As they continue walking, Alison is admiring the Fiesta and then notices a sign in the back window: "For Sale: $3,000 ono". Her heart takes a leap, and she moves closer to check that she is not imagining it.

The driver, Tom has got out of the car and is filling it with fuel. Alison approaches him and asks him about the car. She finds out that it belongs to a friend who has been offered the opportunity of a lifetime in Australia and has had to leave the country suddenly, leaving the car with Tom to sell. Tom and the owner of the car, Alan had shared an apartment, and when Alan had to leave suddenly, it meant that Tom would be left to pay the full rent for a month until he found a new housemate.

Although Alan's share of the rent was only $1,000 he gave Tom the car to sell as compensation for leaving him with everything, including all of the bills and various other things to sort out at the last minute. Since Alan didn't need the car, and his new job in Australia came with a company car and impressive salary, it was his way of making it up to Tom.

Tom had had the car listed for sale for a month, but no-one had bought it. Finally, he found himself in a position where he really needed cash urgently and dropped the price dramatically, hoping he could get a quick sale. Alison had finally found her pale blue Ford Fiesta in excellent condition and for a price she could afford. She had found it, not by looking for it, but by keeping herself in a state of unconditional love, and following what felt good in the moment. If she had forced herself to go and look at the Civic, she may or may not have ended up buying it, but she certainly wouldn't have been at that gas station at that time.

If she hadn't taken a moment to look for her favorite magazine she wouldn't have seen the notice board; and if she hadn't stayed to read the notice board, she and Shanti would have left the gas station earlier and missed Tom's arrival.

Rather than coincidence this synchronicity is the result of consciously choosing to follow what feels good in the moment instead of forcing herself to do what she thought she "should" do. Remaining in a state of unconditional love enabled her to make those decisions.

If she had been feeling disappointed, frustrated or despondent she may not have chosen to go bowling; or, it may have felt better to stay in the car instead of going into the store, which would have resulted leaving earlier. Or, if she did go into the store, she may not have thought to look for her magazine in that negative state, which means she wouldn't have seen the notice board. Or, if she had seen it, she may not have bothered to look at the notice board if she was feeling despondent.

The timing would have been out had she been in a negative state, and she wouldn't have crossed paths with Tom at that time. The combination of remaining in a state of unconditional love and following what feels good in the moment is what allows synchronicity to play out effectively, and lead you to your goal in the easiest, least resistant way.

This does not mean there is only one path to what you want, and if you miss that opportunity you will never get what you want. There will always be another route. But following what feels good is the fastest and easiest route. Doing what you feel you should do instead of what feels good may mean taking a much longer detour on the way to the manifestation of your desire.

In the beginning, it's difficult to stay tuned in to the unconditional bit, and it's natural to keep slipping into conditional love – loving it with the hope or expectation that it will manifest. But it really doesn't take that much practice to master the ability.

The only way to fully understand this is to try it out. It's best to start with small things – minor irritations that don't have consequences. In the "Exercises" chapter, I'll explain in more detail, how to do this.

It's how you feel MOST of the time that determines what you are creating and attracting in your life.

Exercises and Techniques

Beginner's Exercise

The First step in tuning in to your Superpower

This is the easiest way I've found to help people get started. The first goal is to identify the physical feeling of your power, so that you know when you're tuning in. To do this, you'll be using thoughts and imagination. But once you've practiced and become familiar with the sensation, you'll no longer need to use this process, you'll be able to tune in directly.

Beginner's Exercise Steps:

1. Sit comfortably, close your eyes and relax.
2. Think of something or someone you have compassion for. By compassion, I don't mean pity or sympathy, or even empathy, I mean a warmth. It needs to be someone or something you don't have any expectations from. So, for example, it could be a baby, child, or pet.
3. Imagine holding that person or animal in your arms in a hug.
4. Take notice of the feeling – the physical sensation - you have in your chest. It may be constant, or it may come and go; it may waver. Focus fully on that physical sensation. What you're feeling is the sensation of your power coursing through you.
5. Now, imagine that feeling, that sensation, as a light – an energy – and imagine it spreading all the way down to your toes, and up to the top of your head.
6. Finally, imagine that light or energy overflowing from you and filling the room you're in.

That's it. That's the exercise that will get you started on tuning in. It's a different experience for everyone, and it can take time. Remember to think of it as a skill you're learning – like learning to ride a bike or to play an instrument. Adopting that attitude will make it easier, and you'll see faster results.

In the beginning the sensation can feel uncomfortable – again, this depends on the person. I found it very uncomfortable when I first started practicing – it felt like my chest was under pressure and was going to explode if I kept it going too long. It was almost (but not quite) painful. But I discovered, as I kept practicing for a little bit each day, it got easier and easier, until it felt perfectly comfortable and normal.

The feeling of discomfort is only because you're not use to it – like feeling stiff muscles when you first start learning a new physical activity. Think of a sheet of paper that has been rolled up for a long time (most of your life so far). When you unroll it and try to roll it the other way, it will keep springing back to roll the way it's used to being rolled.

It'll take time and consistency to keep rolling it the new way, before it straightens out, and then easily rolls the new way. It's the same with your power. Because most of us are not used to channeling our power - we're used to being without it, and the feelings that go with that – when we start tuning in to it, it can be very uncomfortable and we may not be able to maintain it for very long. But if we keep practicing it consistently, it gets easier and easier.

If you feel this discomfort (and I've found that many people do), hold it for only a few seconds – that's fine to begin with. Then do it again, for just a few seconds, and then build on that. See if you can build up to a minute in the first few days, and then see how much you can increase that in the first week. Because each person is different of course, we all progress at different rates; but for everyone, the more you practice, the faster you'll master it.

Once you're able to hold the sensation (stay tuned in to your power) for at least a minute or two, you can move on to the Superpower Exercise in the next chapter. If you find it too challenging to tune in using that exercise, come back to the Beginner's Exercise until it gets easier, and then move on to the Superpower Exercise.

Have fun with it, enjoy it. Think of yourself as a baby Superman or Superwoman, learning to use your insanely powerful superpower. It's going to take some time, practice and consistency, but how much fun is it to know that you have this power, and you're going to be able to use it to create and attract whatever you want in your life! ☺

Superpower Exercise

The Next Step in Learning to Use Your Superpower

Once you've mastered the Beginner's Exercise, you should be familiar with the sensation you're aiming for. Using something or someone you already feel love and compassion for to pinpoint the physical feeling of your power will give you a guideline. Now we're going to move on to expanding your power – we're going to work on filling yourself with your power so that you are able to aim it at targets in the world around you.

You can't give what you don't have, so the aim of this exercise is to develop your ability to fill yourself with unconditional love for yourself; so that it can then overflow to whatever you wish to improve in the world around you. Now, most people find it challenging to love themselves unconditionally (if at all).

Using the "Look how much I love myself" exercise from the chapter "How Unconditional Love Works with Finances" will help you begin to open up more to this. And this exercise is designed to make it easy to build that unconditional love for yourself in an indirect, but effective way.

Superpower Exercise Steps

1. Sit comfortably, close your eyes, and relax.

2. Think of the person or animal you used in the Beginner's Exercise, and tune in to that physical feeling you were practicing in that exercise.
3. Now, think about the cells in your body. There are approximately 50 trillion cells in your body, each one with a consciousness, and each cell working to the best of its ability, to serve the whole – you. Each of those 50 trillion cells is working to serve you. Doing its best – which is all it knows how to do.
4. Send that feeling – that sensation, that unconditional love - to each of those cells. Imagine them filling up with that energy. Realize that you love them just for being there. Just for existing.
5. Now, pull your focus back a bit – like a camera pulling out to a wider shot – and see your whole body filled with that energy. Your whole body is filled with love just for existing.
6. See that energy filling you right up, and overflowing from you, to fill the room you're in.
7. Imagine someone or something you love, and see them being filled with that energy of unconditional love.
8. Think of a specific reason you love them and feel that feeling intensify.
9. Now, imagine they don't have that trait or quality, and keep that energy going. Keep them filled with that energy even without the reason you love them. For example, one of the things you may love about your dog is that he's really cuddly and affectionate. Now imagine he's not affectionate and in fact doesn't like being cuddled, is always struggling to get away – and love him anyway. Keep him full of that energy of unconditional love.

Another example: One of the things you may love about a friend is that she's always there for you when you need her. Now, imagine she's not available. Imagine she doesn't answer when you call her, she doesn't return your call. And love her anyway. Keep that energy of unconditional love filling her anyway. Take care not to entertain reasons and excuses –

for example "She may be busy" – the important thing is to tune into the "unconditional" bit of your power (which is its potency), so imagine she just didn't get back to you – for no good reason, and keep that energy of unconditional love filling her anyway.

Depending on the individual, the person you chose, and the circumstances of your relationship with that person, it may take a while to get to a point where you're able to do this. It can be a challenge, but keep practicing. Each time you can't keep that feeling of unconditional love going, see it as you've just overbalanced on the bicycle, and you're just going to get back on and try again. Maybe take a little break if you need to, and then try again. You WILL be able to do this, it only takes practice. Keep going.

Practice this exercise every day, at least once a day, so that you keep developing and improving your skill. You may like to start aiming your power at small irritations as well – food you don't like, a song on the radio that irritates you, a red traffic light, the weather. Experiment with it as you practice the exercise, and you'll reach a turning point, where you'll see results.

When you feel ready, move on to the exercises in the following chapters, which give you techniques for using your power on specific issues and challenges. There are many different ways of imagining using your power. You can simply see your "target" being filled with the energy or light; you can imagine you have a water gun filled with your power and imagine drenching your targets in unconditional love; you can imagine you have an "anti-bacterial spray bottle" filled with unconditional love which you can spray at anything and everything. Play around with it, experiment, and find whatever works best for you.

Note: Make sure you're full of your power yourself, before moving on to aiming it at issues and challenges. Spend time using this

Superpower Exercise to fill yourself with unconditional love first. You can't give what you don't have. ;)

Technique for Using Your Superpower on Difficult and Negative People

We all come into contact with people we find difficult, and those who seem to always be negative. It's usually a work colleague, boss, client or family member. But it can also be a friend, acquaintance or even a stranger – perhaps a cashier or shop assistant.

We can't make other people change. Or can we? ;) What we can do, is we can change the settings on the control panel inside ourselves, which controls everything "out there" – in our life experience – including other people. And your Superpower is the way to do this.

As I mentioned before, it's natural to be concerned that if you love negative behavior, you're condoning it, and even encouraging more of it. It's a natural concern, but it's not a valid one. Remember to think of that negativity as darkness, and the power of unconditional love as light. When you shine light into darkness, it doesn't encourage more darkness; it transforms the darkness into light! ☺

What you're doing with your power has nothing to do with the conscious level of communication with the other person. It works on an energetic level, on a quantum level. You are making changes below the surface, so in fact, what you say and do really doesn't matter; it's only how you feel that is making the changes.

Difficult People Technique

1. Sit comfortably, close your eyes, and relax.
2. Use steps 1 to 6 of the Superpower Exercise to tune in to your power.

3. Keep that energy flowing, as you imagine the difficult person.
4. See the energy filling them up completely, from their toes to the top of their head.
5. Imagine them as you wish they would be – imagine the behavior you would like to see from them, and keep that energy going – love that behavior.
6. Now, imagine them exactly as they are – with whatever it is that you don't like about them, and fill that with the energy. Love them anyway. Feel that love for them exactly as they are.
7. Now, love the behavior itself. Remember, by loving it, you're shining light into darkness. The love does need to be unconditional and genuine. You may not be able to manage this at first, but keep practicing, and it will get easier and easier – you will surprise yourself! ☺

Practice this technique to improve your skill – you'll feel the difference as you do it more and more. Once you have managed to tune in and have accomplished step 7, use the technique before you are due to encounter the person; and with practice, you'll find you're able to go directly to Step 7, right in the middle of a conversation with them! I can't describe just how magical that is! ☺

Using Your Superpower To Heal Your Body

As Joseph Murphy explains so brilliantly and thoroughly in his book **THE POWER OF YOUR SUBCONSCIOUS MIND**, healing is a natural and automatic process, and the subconscious is programmed to return the body to a state of peak health.

What happens though is, bearing in mind the effect the way we feel has on our bodies, and considering we spend so much of our lives in a state of worry, anxiety, frustration, resentment, anger, fear, melancholy, and other negative states of mind, we are literally preventing the healing. So, instead of the body getting itself back to its natural state of pure health, it's being blocked from this on an energetic level, but also on a chemical and biological level – by stress hormones and various other chemicals associated with negative emotional states.

When your dominant state is unconditional love, you are channeling your superpower most of the time, and your body is receiving a constant flow of "feel-good" chemicals and hormones. Remember the experiments Gregg Braden describes? Remember the study that featured individuals trained in feelings of love and compassion? The results of feeling those emotions were physical changes in the shape of their DNA.

Braden explains that when DNA is healthy, it is loosely wound; when it is not healthy, it is tightly wound. The study showed that dominant states of love and compassion resulted in those participants' DNA relaxing, loosening (extremely healthy).

Feeling good also boosts the immune system, of course, and nothing feels better than unconditional love. Nothing feels better than having the power of the energy that creates and transforms worlds, coursing through you! ☺

A couple of years ago, I had really bad toothache. My dentist explained it was an abscess, and gave me antibiotics for it. He told me that if those didn't work, or if the abscess returned, the tooth would have to be pulled. This was, of course, not an option I wanted!

The antibiotics worked, and the pain went away. However, a few months later, it was back! The abscess had returned. And this time, the dentist said the tooth needed to be extracted. During the two weeks between the consultation and the tooth-pulling appointment, I decided to use my superpower to heal the abscess instead.

I used the Superpower Exercise, and then whenever I felt the pain, I aimed my power at that area. I loved the abscess even if it never went away. I loved the tooth even if it was going to be extracted. I loved me and my tooth and the abscess, even if this superpower healing thing didn't work.

It worked! Within three days, the pain had subsided, and I cancelled the dentist appointment. And it hasn't returned since!

Jessica's Story *(A True Story)*

Here is a message I received from Jessica, a teenager in Canada I coached through private messages on a forum. Jessica first contacted me to find out if the power of unconditional love could be used for her predicament. She was being bullied at school and was very unhappy. I gave Jessica the exercises detailed in this book, and suggested she use the Superpower Exercise every day before leaving for school. I also recommended that while at school, she use the exercises to keep herself topped up with the power of unconditional love, and aim it at everyone around her.

I received a message from Jessica a few months later saying that her life had completely changed. She had used her superpower as I had suggested, and not only was she no longer being bullied, she was actually popular. She wrote that everyone liked her; she was getting straight "A"s in school, and was involved in various school activities.

I asked Jessica if I could share her story to inspire others, and she agreed. The complete correspondence between us is detailed in the book **"BEYOND THE MAGIC PILL"** if you would like to read more about Jessica, the changes she achieved, and how she achieved them.

Once Jessica had experienced that massive achievement – changing her experience of others in such a dramatic way - she continued to use the power of unconditional love for further goals, including making physical changes.

What follows is her account of some of the changes she achieved, in her own words. It is important to bear in mind that when Jessica sent the following message to me, she had been practicing using her superpower consistently and intensely for a long time. It does take persistence, practice and patience in order to develop the skill to the level Jessica has reached.

Having said that, her story is incredibly inspiring, and will give you an idea of what is possible for you to achieve if you put in the practice and are persistent. Putting in the same amount of time, practice and effort that you would put in to learning to play an instrument or learning a new language will help you to achieve the most magical results.

Here is Jessica's message:

" Hey everythings good!! =)

Sure I'd be happy to share the details, so I made a few physical changes. First I started off with skin so I sent unconditional love every day to my body and skin, and for the first two months I saw some small changes, then after, I saw big faster changes. My skin changed dramatically week after week. After, I worked on my body. I wanted to eat anything and not diet or exercise and I sent unconditional love and it worked. This took three weeks. The biggest change was my eye sight. I sent unconditional love, and overnight my vision got perfect!!

This one surprised me!! After, I made some small changes. I removed a scar on my leg and I worked on changing my face shape. This also took about two weeks. I noticed when I changed my eye sight I was very positive about the change and had no resistance so I think that's why it happened overnight. Another thing I noticed was when I tried making my first physical change it took time, but after a couple of months of practice my changes were a lot faster. So yeah, those are changes I did. Hope this helped!! Love You!!" – Jessica Fontana, Toronto

Technique for Healing the Body Using Your Superpower

Healing your body using your superpower works in the same way it works for other topics. Use the Superpower Exercise to fill yourself with unconditional love for yourself (this step is even more important when healing the body, of course), and then aim that power at whatever is ailing you.

Healing the Body Technique – Step-by-Step

1. Fill yourself with unconditional love for yourself, using the Superpower Exercise.
2. Once you're full of your power, think of the part of your body that needs healing, and focus on sending your power to that part particularly.
3. Imagine that part of your body as perfect – completely healed and in perfect health, and fill that version of it with your power.
4. Now see it exactly as it is, and love it anyway. Keep that love going; keep it filled up with that love, exactly as it is right now. If it's painful, love it anyway. Love the pain (this may sound absurd or impossible, but it only takes practice, and you'll find it actually becomes perfectly easy to send love to the pain). Love it completely, exactly as it is, without expecting it to change. Love it even if it never heals. That is where the power is!

Again, the more you do this, the easier it will become, and the more impressive the results. In fact, in order to keep yourself in a constant state of good health, keep yourself topped up with your power by tuning in regularly, using the Superpower Exercise.

Using Your Superpower for Health
How to change your exercise and eating habits

You can use your Superpower to achieve your ideal body weight, and to become fit and healthy. Use the Superpower Exercise to fill your body with unconditional love, and then keep that love going, for your body even if it never changes. Love it exactly as it is (remember, you're shining a light into darkness). Love the bits you wish would change; love them exactly as they are. Even if they never change, you love them anyway.

Your Superpower and Healthy Eating – Steps

1. Tune into your power using the Superpower Exercise.
2. Think of the food you wish you would eat – the healthy food you wish you liked more.
3. Imagine your power overflowing from you, and filling that food
4. Now, imagine you're eating unhealthy food – whatever your favorites are, and fill that food with your power. Fill yourself and the unhealthy food, and the fact that you're eating it, with love even though you're unable to resist it. Love it all anyway.

As you progress, using this power, you'll find your desire for healthy food increases, while your desire for unhealthy food decreases – if you love it all unconditionally. In other words, when you do find yourself giving in to temptation, make sure you use your superpower to fill yourself, the food, and the fact that you're eating it, with unconditional love. The way you feel has more of an effect on your body that the food you're eating. And the more you use your power on yourself and all food, the more you'll find your desire changing to become healthier.

Your Superpower and Exercise – Steps

1. Use the Superpower Exercise to tune in to your power, and fill yourself with unconditional love for yourself.
2. Imagine yourself doing whatever exercise it is you wish you would do, and fill that version of you with love. See your power filling you up as you are running, or exercising in the gym, or swimming, or whatever it is you would like to do.
3. Now, imagine yourself not doing any exercise. Imagine yourself doing whatever it is you normally do instead of exercising. And love that too! Fill that version of yourself with the same power – love the fact that you're not exercising. Keep that same feeling going.
4. When you choose not to exercise, in that moment, tune into your power. When you feel disappointed or critical, or worried, or any other negative feelings about not exercising, stop right in the middle of those feelings, and use the Superpower Exercise to tune in to your power, and fill yourself with your superpower. And then aim it at the fact that you didn't exercise. Love yourself anyway, and love the fact that you didn't exercise.

The result will be that you start noticing you have more energy and less resistance to exercising. The important thing is to keep aiming your power at what you don't want, and to keep reminding yourself that in doing that you are aiming light at darkness.

Technique for Fear and Anxiety

In the chapter on how your Superpower works with finances, I spoke about the fact that you don't need to learn to love yourself – you already do. All you need to do is remember that you love yourself, and start to notice, recognize and acknowledge the evidence of that love. Noticing the small things around you, and commenting to yourself "Look how much I love myself!" is a life-transforming exercise.

Now I'm going to add to that concept, something that will help you to no long feel fear or anxiety. Once you know you love yourself, you cannot create or attract anything bad for yourself. Think about it. If you love someone, you protect them, and you would never hurt them. Since you now know that you love yourself, it's impossible for you to create or attract ANYTHING bad for you.

Sometimes things may appear to be bad, it may look like something is wrong, but if you remind yourself - "Now that I know I love myself, I can only attract situations and people that feel good, and that are good for me" - you will find that fear and anxiety eventually subside and disappear.

Have you ever been in a dark room (perhaps when you were a child) and seen something in the gloom that you could swear was something else – you could swear it's a person or a monster, and you can't imagine it could be anything else. And then you switch the light on, and it turns out it's a robe on the back of the door, or a lamp, or a bag, or a coat. But before you switched the light on you were absolutely certain it was something sinister.

This is what the "bad stuff" is in your life now. No matter what it looks like, you can remind yourself that, since you now know that you love yourself, it's impossible for you to create anything but good for yourself. So, even though whatever it is may look like something bad, it can't be; it HAS to turn out to be good, or at the very least, nothing to worry about; because that's all you're capable of creating and attracting now.

Combined with this, aiming your superpower at whatever it is you're worried about will "turn the light on" for you, so you will see that what looked like a monster is in fact just a robe, or a lamp… or maybe even a surprise gift. And again, the more you practice this, the less often you'll feel fear, worry and anxiety; and even when you do occasionally feel it, it won't be intense and it won't last for long.

Exercise for Reducing Fear – Steps:

1. Fill yourself with unconditional love for yourself using the Superpower Exercise.
2. Imagine whatever it is you're worried about, and fill it with that power.
3. Imagine the worst that could happen – so, if you're worried about bills you can't pay, for example, imagine what will happen if you never get the money to pay them, the worst case scenario – and fill that outcome with your power. Love the fact that you can't pay the bill, and love the outcome.
4. Use your power to fill everyone involved, with unconditional love. Love the whole situation. Remember, the thing you're worried about is darkness, and your power of unconditional love is light. In loving the worst case scenario, you are shining light into the darkness, and that is how you transform darkness to light! ☺

Use this exercise whenever you feel worried or anxious; and combine it with reminding yourself that no matter what things may look like, now that you know you love yourself, you are only capable of creating and attracting things that feel good and that are good for you. So it has to turn out to be either good, or nothing to worry about.

This may seem like a bit of a stretch, and you may not be able to see right now, how it can work, but I encourage you to just try it. Just start with the steps below, even if you don't believe it yet, and see what happens. It doesn't cost anything but a little focus and attention; and the effect this exercise has on how you feel will surprise you!

If you find yourself in a state of worry or anxiety often, I recommend practicing the self-love exercise throughout your day, as much as possible. This is where you notice all the good stuff, and recognize it as an expression of love from yourself, to yourself (because you are the one who creates and attracts in your life), and use the phrase "Look how much I love myself".

Put signs and sticky notes up around your home or office to remind yourself to do this, or you could set an alarm in your phone at various times throughout the day, as a reminder.

Here are a few examples of little things you could use for this exercise, to give you an idea of the wide variety of options available to you:

- It's sunny (Look how much I love myself!)
- There are birds tweeting (Look how much I love myself)
- Beautiful flowers or blossoms (Look how much I love myself)
- A convenient parking spot (Look how much I love myself)
- I have a computer (Look how much I love myself)

- I have electricity and running water (Look how much I love myself)
- A smile from a stranger (Look how much I love myself)
- The traffic light turned green as I approached the intersection (Look how much I love myself)
- A call from a friend (Look how much I love myself)
- My favorite song on the radio (Look how much I love myself)
- Something that made me laugh (Look how much I love myself)

And the list could go on and on of course. You can see from this list, there are endless opportunities to recognize and acknowledge expressions of love from yourself, to yourself. And the more you do this, the more the idea will sink in that you love yourself and you can therefore only create and attract good for yourself. Combine this with using your superpower on anything you are worried about, and you'll be fearless in no time! ☺

I can't remember the last time I felt fear or anxiety. Well, of course there have been glimpses for a moment, but literally only a moment, and then they're gone. And do you know, since I started using this technique, years ago, I haven't once had anything "bad" happen to me. Even things that looked like they may be bad turned out to be either good, or nothing to worry about!

Technique for "Broken" Things

This is pretty amazing; and if I hadn't experienced myself, I'd have a hard time believing it. I've had several situations where something has appeared to be broken, or damaged, and then turned out just fine after I've used the Superpower.

The first time this happened was right in the very beginning, when I first discovered this power. And it's one of the events that gave me such complete faith in it. If it could do this, it could do anything, and it is certainly a true superpower!

I was on my way to my very first singing gig. I was very nervous, but had done my pre-paving before leaving home. I had filled myself, the venue, and everyone in it, with unconditional love before I left the house. It was a four-hour gig, about 40 minutes' drive from where I lived, and I was going to be using backing tracks, which were on my iPod.

On the drive to the venue, at a point in the journey when it was too late to go back, I realized that I had forgotten to charge my iPod! My heart nearly jumped out of my throat. It had some charge, but nowhere near enough to last four hours. I then remembered I had a charger with me, so I planned to plug it in when I reached the venue.

I forgot! When I got to the venue, it was so packed and chaotic (all good – great crowd, in a fabulous party mood) and I was distracted, and completely forgot about the iPod. I only remembered again at the beginning of the last set; in the fourth hour of the gig. The battery indicator was on red, and it was about to die. I couldn't plug it in while using it, as it was one of those iPods that won't play while charging.

So, I did the only thing I could do, I ignored the fear of it dying in the middle of a song, in the middle of this crowded venue where people were loving the music and dancing. I ignored my fear of the people being upset and the venue manager being furious and never hiring me again... and instead, I used my superpower on it.

Right in the middle of singing, I sent unconditional love to the iPod. I filled it with love – even if it did stop in the middle of a song; even if the people hated me; and even if the management refused to pay me and never hired me again. No matter what happened, I loved it anyway.

It not only lasted the rest of that hour,ced for the four encores as well! There is no way it should have lasted. But it did. That sold me on the power of unconditional love. From then on, I was an unshakable believer! ☺

One of my coaching clients recently transformed a broken portable AC unit in this way. It was 40 degrees in Delhi at the time, and Snigdha and her family were sweltering. They have a personal cooler (portable air conditioning unit) which had been in storage. They retrieved it from storage and cleaned it up, looking forward to some relief from the oppressive heat. However, when they switched the unit on, it wasn't working.

Overcoming the disappointment and frustration of having tinkered with it, trying to get it to work with no luck, Snigdha used her superpower, filling herself with unconditional love first, and then aiming it at the cooler. She filled the cooler with the energy of unconditional love, loving it even if it wasn't going to work; even if it never worked.

She then went back to tinkering with it a little, and, although she had tried everything before with no success, the cooler began working after she had used her superpower. And it continued to work, saving her from having to call in an electrician.

Now, there have been times I've used it on broken or damaged things and it hasn't made them work again, but the situation has always still turned out perfectly anyway.

Using Unconditional Love on Inanimate Objects – Steps

1. At the time you discover something's wrong, stop whatever you're trying to do physically with thing, and sit quietly for a moment with your eyes closed, and relax.
2. Use the Superpower Exercise to fill yourself with unconditional love for yourself.
3. Imagine that energy overflowing from you, to the object concerned, and see it filling that object.
4. Imagine the object is perfect. Imagine it working perfectly, and keep that energy of love flowing into it.
5. Now, imagine the object will never be fixed. Imagine it is broken and is unfixable, or is going to cost a fortune to have repaired, and love it anyway. Keep that energy of unconditional love flowing into it. Love it exactly as it is, right now, in its "brokenness".

Remember, the power is in the unconditional bit. Be sure you are loving it even if it stays exactly as it is. If you find it does actually stay exactly as it is, continue to love it anyway; and fill whatever steps need to be taken with unconditional love as well. In addition to this, fill anyone involved with unconditional love too. And you'll find that no matter what happens, and even if it looks bad, it will turn out to be good, or at the very least, nothing to worry about!

Power Phrases

When you have mastered the Beginner's and Superpower Exercises, you will be ready to tune into your power without using those processes. You will be able to literally "flick a switch" to turn on your power.

Although I recommend still using the Superpower Exercise regularly, as a maintenance and "top-up" tool, it is very useful to be able to tune in to your power instantly as well.

One of the tools that can help you to develop this skill is using a power phrase. You don't need power phrases, but they can help in the beginning, while you are still developing your skill. Power phrases are also very effective when you are finding it challenging to tune in to your power in a particular situation or with a specific person.

I'm going to share with you, a few that I use, but you can make up your own. The idea behind the power phrase is that the brain has linked it with the state your body gets into when you're channeling your power; and so, when you say the phrase, your body automatically goes into that state.

It can be as meaningful as "I love you" or as obscure as "sausages". As long as you prepare by going through the exercise that links the word or phrase to the state of unconditional love in the brain, it doesn't matter what the actual phrase or word is.

I often use the Ho'oponopono phrase "I'm sorry, please forgive me, I forgive you, thank you, I love you" – this is powerful for me because it's one of the two main sources of my insight on unconditional love. It was

Ho'oponopono (through Joe Vitale and Ihaleakala Hew Len's book "Zero Limits") and that phrase, along with Klaus Joehle's "Living on Love" book that led me to discover this power.

So I often still use that phrase now, when I need to tune in quickly in a particularly challenging situation. And it works brilliantly. I also add the SGI Buddhist chant "Nam Myoho Renge Kyo" on the end. So I'll say "I'm sorry, please forgive me, I forgive you, thank you, I love you. Nam Myoho Renge Kyo" – and that is full of unconditional love! ☺

You could just repeat "I love you" or "Thank you" or you could use one of the power phrases I've created – which are also very effective, and I still use them myself: "No matter what happens, I love the part of me that is creating this experience", and for those particularly frustrating times, when you find you're too negative to be positive, here's a fun sarcastic version of that one – which helps to lighten the mood in a funny way: "I love the part of me that is creating this sh*t... er, I mean, experience." It won't tune you into unconditional love, but it'll lighten you a little from where you are. And from there you'll be closer to tuning in. A little humor can be very powerful! ☺

How to Use Power Phrases

The purpose of power phrases is to act as a trigger for when you're not in a position to be able to go through the Superpower Exercise. It is very effective when you want to tune in to your power instantly, in the moment, and you're having some trouble tuning in.

To clarify: You will be able to simply turn your power on most of the time, without having to use a power phrase; but power phrases help you to make the transition from the Superpower Exercise to being able to tune in without the process. They also help in those times when you are in an emotional state that is hindering you from tuning in directly.

1. Program the power phrase by using it during your Superpower Exercise. While you're feeling the feeling of unconditional love, repeat the power phrase over and over. Do this whenever you do the Superpower Exercise.
2. When you "take the training wheels off" by starting to practice conjuring up the feeling of unconditional love without the Superpower Exercise, repeat the phrase as you tune in.
3. Whenever you find yourself in a state that is making it difficult for you to tune in, repeat the phrase to yourself, as you tune in. It will give you a "leg up" ☺

When You Can't Feel Love

Being human, there will be times, even once you've become an expert in using your power, when you can't feel unconditional love... or any kind of love. It is part of the human experience to have challenges and contrast, and sometimes you will feel how you feel and not be able to tune in to your power. So what do you do then? Love the fact that you can't feel love! ☺

Remember, the potency in your Superpower is in the unconditional bit. And of course, unconditional means no condition. And it applies to your not being able to feel unconditional love as well as everything else! It's a bit odd, but it's true and it works. At those times you cannot tune in, love the fact that you can't tune in. Once you get used to using your power regularly, you'll realize you can aim it at absolutely everything and anything – even at yourself when you can't tune in to it!

You'll also sometimes forget to use it. Especially in the beginning, because it's a new thing, you will often forget to use it. So, you'll experience something, react in the way you're used to reacting, and then afterwards realize that you could have used your power on it. In those instances you may feel frustrated with yourself for forgetting; and that's okay.

Right then, as you remember it, tune in and fill yourself with your power. Love yourself for forgetting. And if you can't love yourself for forgetting at that time, love the fact that you can't love yourself for forgetting! Remember, unconditional love is light. By loving the fact that you can't love, you're shining light into darkness, which will transform it to light.

So, no matter what is going on, there's always an option to use your power, to love. Even if it's loving the fact that you can't use your power… which is using your power! ☺

All of this may seem peculiar until you start using it. It'll all make sense when you try it!

More Techniques and Tips for Tuning In

Over the years, I've discovered more and more techniques for tuning in, in various situations; and I know that once you start using your power, you'll find many more of your own. Here are a few that have worked for me. Try them, and see how effective they are for you. You may like to adjust them, and they may also give you some ideas of your own.

Connecting with Beauty

I discovered – not long ago actually – that no matter what is happening around you, focusing on something beautiful and connecting with it can help you to tune in to your power in the moment. I found that colors are amazingly effective for this. Sitting in traffic, worrying about being late and feeling stressed?

Gaze at the bright red brake lights of the car in front of you – focus on the vibrancy of the color, and connect with it. And as you do this, tune in to your power, and aim it at that beautiful bright red. See how long you can stay connected. Then, aim your power at the traffic, the fact that you are running late, and any potential consequences. Think of the worst case scenario, and fill that outcome with love. Love it all anyway, no matter how it turns out.

Doing this exercise and loving whatever the outcome will be, will mean it will have to turn out well, regardless of how it may appear in the current moment. You can use anything within your sight for this exercise. If you are in a building, look around you and find something you can focus on and appreciate. A painting, the color of the carpet, even a plain white wall will do. Gazing at a plain white wall, focusing on, and appreciating the whiteness of it can take you into a calm state from which you can begin to tune in to your power.

Try it out with different focal points whenever you think of it, to see how it works for you. You don't need to wait until you feel stressed or worried, practice it throughout your day and you'll be amazed at the results.

The Inner Hug

This technique is extremely powerful, and can be used anytime, anywhere! Imagine you're hugging the inside of you – just as you would hug a loved one. It can seem weird at first, but once you've done it, it becomes perfectly normal and easy. You don't need to do anything physically with your arms; just imagining you are hugging yourself will create a feeling in your chest and a chemical reaction in your brain.

This is a great exercise to use throughout the day; and because it's quick and there's nothing visual going on, you can literally do it anywhere, under any circumstances. It may seem simplistic, but do try it – you'll be surprised at just how effective it is.

Points to Remember

You are now armed with everything you need, to make the most of the infinite possibilities open to you through using your superpower. I hope you are as excited as I am for you! ☺ There is nothing you can't achieve, and nothing to be afraid of now that you are in command of your power.

I advise going through this book regularly, and re-reading the chapters that apply specifically to your own circumstances and challenges. You will learn and understand new insights and aspects each time you do this. It takes repetitive exposure to new concepts, for the mind to fully comprehend them. It is amazing how much information falls out of our heads even once we believe we know it! ☺

There are a few points that are particularly important to remember:

It is worth writing these points on notes and placing them where you will see them regularly, as reminders since it is easy to forget this information in the middle of dealing with everyday life.

1. Learning to use your power is like learning to ride a bicycle, play an instrument or learning to speak a new language. Like any skill it takes practice.
2. Loving what you don't want is shining a light into darkness. It will release the darkness, transforming it into light.
3. When you find you are unable to feel love, love the fact that you can't feel love. It sounds impossible, but you'll find that with practice it is easier than you might expect.

4. Your power is inside you, all you need to do is learn to master it.

In Closing…

For more from me…

Visit my website and blog at: www.yourselfempowered.com where you will find more information, tools and techniques as well as details of my live events.

Apart from sharing my techniques for tuning in to and using the power of unconditional love through my books, I also deliver keynote speeches on the subject and related topics. I specialize specifically in live training sessions in which I teach and guide participants through the process of developing the ability to use their superpower for all sorts of challenges, issues and goals.

If you would like to find out more about booking me for a keynote speech or training session, or if you would like to attend one of my regular training sessions, please contact me either through my website, or through the **BEYOND THE MAGIC PILL** Facebook page at: https://www.facebook.com/beyondthemagicpill

I hope to meet you at one of my events one day, but until then, should you have any questions, comments or queries, I would love to hear from you either through my blog or the Facebook page above.

Enjoy your superpower and use it liberally!

Love and Light and Magic
Odille xxx

Further Reading and Education

The information in this book will give you the tools you need in order to develop the ability to use your power effectively. The most difficult aspects about using your power are: remembering to practice using it, and "getting back on the bike to keep going when you fall off."

With practice and consistency you will master your skill to such an extent you will feel as though you have a magic power at your fingertips; and that is essentially what it is. The power is already in you, all you need to do, by using the exercises I've shared with you here, is practice consistently. That's all.

Having said that, if you would like to learn more about how your subconscious works, the Law of Attraction, or Ho'oponopono, I recommend the following. Combine each of these with your superpower, and you will be unstoppable!

Bob Proctor's "Hidden Self Image" and Unconditional Love

If you haven't yet watched Bob Proctor's videos on YouTube on the hidden self-image, I highly recommend them. Bob describes the core explanation for why we get the results we get in life even when we try as hard as we can to change our behavior. The great news is: Bob also explains how you can make the changes to the "hidden self-image" that will result in automatic changes occurring in your life.

The information Bob shares explains the easy way to change habits and results in all areas of your life. Use your superpower in conjunction with Bob's teachings for the most powerful results. As you make the changes using Bob's teachings, whenever you find yourself reverting back to your "old self" fill that old self with unconditional love. Fill it with love exactly as it is. You'll find the changes much easier!

Abraham-Hicks

YouTube is full of videos featuring Ester Hicks and Abraham. If you are interested in learning more about the Law of Attraction, Abraham-Hicks is, in my view, the highest authority on the subject. Search for the videos on YouTube, and visit their website: www.abraham-hicks.com to benefit from a wealth of knowledge and insight. Use your superpower to get yourself into the "Vortex" as well as onto the "High-flying disk".

Ho'oponopono

For more information on the ancient Hawaiian practice of Ho'oponopono, visit http://hooponopono.org/ You can also find a great guide on this practice in the book **ZERO LIMITS** by Joe Vitale and Dr. Hew Len. You will find more information on the book here: www.zerolimits.info

Gregg Braden with more on The Science of Feelings

As I mentioned in the beginning of this book, there is scientific evidence of the connection between all things. Experiments and studies have shown how the way we feel directly affects the world and people around us on a quantum level.

For details on these experiments and studies, search for Gregg Braden on YouTube. There are some excellent videos in which he explains the science brilliantly.

You can also find his website at: http://www.greggbraden.com

Printed in Great Britain
by Amazon